Love Means...

"Love isn't something you find.
Love is something that finds
you."

Loretta Young

The most heartfelt thoughts
from 30 people on what love
means to them.

+ 20 Classic quotes

Love Means...

createspace publishing / Amazon
First published in 2016 by createspace ltd
Text and Illustrations copyright
© R J Gregory 2016

ISBN-13: 978-1530877560
ISBN-10: 1530877563

100% of the royalties earned from
this book will go directly to the
British Heart Foundation

Registered Charity No: 225971

Love Means...

For Jodie

You are my world, my
inspiration, and my light in
the darkness.

*"The sweetest of all sounds is
that of the voice of the woman
we love."*

Jean de la Bruyere

Love Means...

"Love seeketh not itself to please, nor for itself hath any care, but for another gives its ease, and builds a Heaven in Hell's despair."

William Blake

Compiled by R. J. Gregory

This book contains romantic and heartfelt quotes from 30 very special people, like you and me, on what they think about love and what it means to them, also 20 classic quotes that have stood the test of time.

The quotes are anonymous and in no particular order. They follow no pattern and no agenda – just complete honesty, straight from the heart. If that wasn't lovely enough, 100% of the royalties earned from this book will go directly to the British Heart Foundation.

Love Means...

"If I had a flower for every time I thought of you ... I could walk through my garden forever."

Alfred Tennyson

Love Means...

"Love to me is a hand to hold
when you need it most"

"Love is someone making you feel
like you are the only person in
the world"

"Love survives through the worst of situations, and thrives through hope. Even when things seem hopeless, love will find its way."

"... seeing the twinkle in her eye after she smiles"

"Love is not being able to experience anything without wishing the other person was there to see it too"

"...coming home to a smile after a long day at work"

"What does love mean to me?
The first time you hear the
word 'Daddy' come out of your
child's mouth and your heart
melts"

"...chocolate and wine – one day
diamonds and yachts!"

"...being treated like a princess"

"Love is... Waking up to find it's not just a dream"

"Love feels like I'm a unicorn, dancing through a meadow."

"Love is having somebody to share things with, someone to eat sushi with, and someone to check things out with."

"Love is to me, when you see your sister's lips open and say 'I love you' and you know she means it."

"Love is when you have P, Marlin, and Joda [my lovely cats and sister] all in the same room together"

"When someone else's happiness becomes your happiness, that is love."

"Love is when you look into someone's eyes and you see their heart."

"Love is a friendship you can't live without."

"Love is accepting someone else's imperfections as perfect and creating a bubble of happiness between yourselves."

"Love is a meeting of two souls, fully accepting the dark and light within each other, bound by the courage to grow through struggle into bliss."

"Love is not about how much you say 'I love you', but how much you can prove it's true."

"Love is just a word, until someone comes along and gives it meaning."

"True love never dies; it just gets stronger with time."

"If someone was standing in front of us with a gun. And there's me and this other person, I would quite happily take that bullet for that person, that's how I know I really love someone."

"Love is a deep feeling of warmth – it is unconditional and can last forever."

"Love is laughter and Prosecco!"

"Love is a shelter from all of life's struggles"

"Love is composed of a single soul inhabiting two bodies."

"Love means knowing that no matter what, you have someone to count on. It's unconditional and makes you feel good on the inside. You can trust the person you love and comfortable around them. It's like your heart tells you that it is good for you!"

"Love is dancing with two feet,

love is finding your heart beat,

love is that feeling you have on
stage,

love is everywhere it will never
go away!"

"When you love what you have,
you have everything you need."

"Every heart sings a song, incomplete, until another heart sings back."

"Love to me is family, it's unconditional, unfathomable and unending."

"Love is feeling a warm glow inside when you think of that special someone."

"Love is only being happy when she is around..."

"Love is having my perfect
daughters with me."

"Love is contentment."

Classic Quotes

"It is not a lack of love, but a lack of friendship that makes unhappy marriages."

Friedrich Nietzsche

"At the touch of love everyone becomes a poet."

Plato

"Being deeply loved by someone gives you strength, while loving someone deeply gives you courage."

Lao-Tzu

"We are shaped and fashioned by those we love."

Goethe

"You don't love someone for their looks, or their clothes, or for their fancy car, but because they sing a song only you can hear."

Oscar Wilde

"Where there is love there is life."

Mahatma Gandhi

"All you need is love. But a little chocolate now and then doesn't hurt."

Charles Schulz

"One word frees us of all the weight and pain of life: That word is love."

Sophocles

"Immature love says: 'I love you because I need you.' Mature love says 'I need you because I love you.'"

Erich Fromm

"Love is an irresistible desire to be irresistibly desired."

Robert Frost

"I would rather have eyes that cannot see; ears that cannot hear; lips that cannot speak, than a heart that cannot love."

Robert Tizon

"Love is a fruit in season at all times, and within reach of every hand."

Mother Teresa

"Tell me who admires you and loves you, and I will tell you who you are."

Antoine De Saint-Exupéry

"In dreams and in love there are no impossibilities."

János Arany

"Other men it is said have seen
angels, but I have seen thee and
thou art enough."

George Moore

"For you see, each day I love
you more. Today more than
yesterday and less than
tomorrow."

Rosemonde Gerard

"To love and win is the best thing. To love and lose, the next best."

William Makepeace Thackeray

"People will forget what you said. People will forget what you did. But people will never forget how you made them feel."

Maya Angelou

"Love is not a matter of counting the years... But making the years count."

Michelle Amand

"I love you. I am at rest with you. I have come home."

Dorothy L. Sayers

With HUGE thanks to everybody who took the time to create a quote for this book!

Your displays of kindness and willingness to show your feelings are a warm reminder that love really is all around us.